GROWING
SMALLER

GROWING SMALLER

Coreen Davis Hampson

Flowstone Press

FLOWSTONE
PRESS

First Flowstone Press Edition • October 2018
ISBN 978-1-945824-20-3

for my grandchildren
**Luca Randall, Lena Randall,
Oscar, Eli and Asa Lundberg,
Josie Switzer, and Gabriel Hampson**
so that some day, when evaluating their family histories,
they can note that their grandmother
once published a book of poetry

and to my husband
Scott Hampson
who encouraged me
almost nightly in this endeavor.

contents

part one

part two

part three

part four

part five

part six

part seven

part eight

Whoever you are, no matter how lonely,
the world offers itself to your imagination,
. . . announcing your place
in the family of things.

Mary Oliver

part one

AFTER THE CRESCENDO

"I'm really getting bigger," Lena says, scrambling through the
woods to the creek. Her four-year-old voice affirms the pride of
accumulation, of chubby hands
tying shoes, of climbing trees
like a monkey,
of saying the "R" in "water."

In glory we are born,
climb through green change
to a golden crescendo
of confounding growth.
Lost in the jungle there,
we hear voices call from all directions where loss disguises as bright
birds.

I say she will be Lena, queen of the jungle, some day.
She says, "I don't want to be
queen of the jungle.
I just want to be the jungle."
"I'll go with you," I say.
"I'm really getting smaller."

HUMMINGBIRD ON DAPHNE

So small, so bare
on this soggy spring day,
like a prayer from long ago
finally heard, and saying
that nothing has really changed
in my seventy-one years.

The fragrance defined my childhood home.
I have worshipped Daphne all my life,
pampered it in the many yards
of my adulthood, just to receive this message:
that I have not changed.

Despite my many wrongs, despite
the rise of mean despots to the throne
of my only homeland, the hummingbird returns
to drink the nectar on this cold day,
as I march around the yard shivering
in my big coat and gloves.

AWAKE

I awoke from dark dreams, swallowed by
the bright warble and whistles of birds —
a song woven of the present.
Suddenly, as always, a cloud burst
and tears of the sky washed clean
the lava rocks
and my brain.

Past achings, after all, live
in the deepest dark of night.
Unless they are searched out.

Today's searching is for
brilliant fish in the clear salt water
and green sea turtles —
new life, and love, for an old heart.

The tower of a grey cloud,
fringed in white,
rises toward the sun, stretching
steadily upward to the moment
when it can burst and
wash away the sand in our eyes.

EIGHT-DOLLAR MOUNTAIN IN MAY

The wild azaleas swallow me,
alone in their meadow.
Overwhelmed by fragrance,
I slide down a creamy funnel
surrounded by petals and stamens,
almost pink.
A faintly conscious spell
sucks me through the green stem,
into the wood.
I long for the deep wet ground,
the source.
I long to wait there
to be born again some spring.

THANK YOU, DAUGHTER

It must have been the music that reminded me —
this strange Andean rhythm
(from the bottom of my box of tapes)
that makes me want to dance.

You and your friends, twenty-ish,
didn't dance.
I, in my bolder forties,
moved my feet a bit to find the beat.
I was invited out on the floor
by a wild-looking African man
with a leopard hat.
He smelled sweaty and had
a beautiful smile.
He knew the rhythms.

It was the best time dancing
I've ever had.
I didn't even thank you for getting me there,
to that high mountain town.
That was your boldness.

RED LOVE

I love the manzanita
for her exotic taste in color.
Deep red of her outer wood,
the hue of dry blood,
paints her as a stranger.
She stands on dry mounds
among fir and pine
like a visitor who may
soon walk away.

Her gray-green leaves
tinged with pink in the spring
hang like thin coins on green limbs
whose red is barely hidden.
Tiny pink blossoms hang in clusters
of teardrops that
gracefully break my heart.

Soon they will round into berries,
dangle over the drying ground, and
wait for pink to green
and green to redden.

HOT TUB MEDITATION

Breathe to the rhythm of the waves.
Let the wind and clouds fill your mind,
replacing the jabber that was there.
The jabber — fantasies, stories
that are not entirely true
glorifying a self that doesn't exist.
You have an Idol who loves this self;
this self loves the Idol.

Skip the Idol if you can, though
he is beautiful, irresistible.
The air of the universe will fill you.
It brings a Presence that is real,
it can fill you if you let it.
Breathe the air and the light.
Make yourself into a flower.

AT SEVENTY

Today I brought a bouquet of fragrant wild roses into the house
and set it on the kitchen table.
Earwigs by the dozen spilled from the delicate petals.
Scattered in every direction.

I had to simply walk away, outside.
Not knowing what to do I did nothing.

Let them go where they will.

Let the cherries ripen and fall, the birds taking their share.
One small pie will be enough this year.

Let the roses stand and die on the stem.
The deadheads tell the story better than nothing.
Let the lawn give way to Buttercups,
and Moles offer up the richest river loam around their holes.
I will carry it in buckets to my plots of squash and beans.
Let the blackberry suckers build an impenetrable fort
around their fruit, and the figs and plums fall,
ferment upon the ground
so the yellow jackets can enjoy their feast.

Let the world grow in around me
that that I may recede into uselessness.

AUTUMN RIVER

Autumn river holds the golden trees,
dying salmon, gentle moving sky.
I wish that I was her cold underlining,
always holding babes and old, old women;
know the coldest cold, and rejoice the summer
like hot Christmas rum.
Autumn river holds old Indian souls
and young yearnings waiting
for the springtime.

Autumn river's babes wait in silence
to be born, and then prepare to die.
I wish that I was her worn, rocky lining,
always waiting for their cold returning.

DAISY CHAIN

the beads dance along in their blue and red skirts,
each one a flower.
two by two, and three by three
arms entwined
feet beating music out of the dusty earth.

circle round
the white bird.
the bride.

their circle joins another;
four arms link them with their blue sleeves.

the knots connecting the chains do not tie
simply to the next bead.
they lead back to the row behind — blue grandfathers — then up to the
row ahead — the red babies,
then back to meet again, where the knot is made;
where all join hands and circle white and new
around the world.
add another daisy to the chain. repeat the pattern.
add one red link and go back one more generation
to tie your knot each time and you will find peace.
do this once a year
and you will make peace in the world.
you will know all your relations.

AIR CONDITIONING

I hear old-time music in the air-
conditioner humming in our suburban home.
It's the binary rhythm of a reel or a hornpipe —
of two feet keeping balance, all alone.
Then balance with your partner,
then balance in a square.
That's the music in the air.

Machinery doesn't waltz.
Romance is not in its program.

This music is a hoedown going
somewhere at a steady pace.

DEVOLUTION

When I was a woman, I dreamed I was a bear
following bright berries down the mountain.
I bit into some plastic pipe full of
the sound of bees, and found that it was only water.
I lay down under a live oak tree.
Dreamed I was a fox
prowling down by the river, hiding
under blackberry bushes, fragrant in the sun.
I like to jump to high places:
my neighbor's hot tub
to shit. Lay back down
under those bushes.
Dreamed I was
a spring Chinook, swimming
uphill over rocks.
Man, it was hard!
Saw a big worm hanging from a hook.
I wasn't hungry.
Laid some eggs in the gravel.
Dreamed I was
a bluejay singing on a willow limb
watching my neighbor mow the grass.
Watching his dog,
the bowl of kibbles —
thinking, "I'll steal one
when he's not looking." Instead
fell asleep to the mower motor.
Dreamed I was a worm in the warm garden dirt
blindly finding my way back to the womb.

EVENING SOUNDS

Crickets stop at the passage of a fox.
Hum of traffic filters through the tangle
of the woods.
Moaning geese return to the field of food
after the daily migration.

A neighbor's horse whinnies for dinner.

Long breath of wind excites the trees to dance,
exhaling the tales of a journey and
celebrating arrival in a rise of yellow leaves.

Your footsteps by the door
hesitate, your voice telling me
news of the war.

But once outside, you forget
and let the crickets resume
their dominion over evening.

Buzzards float silently
over the top of things.

FIRST RAIN

Woke up in the drought of a dry night's sleep,
after trudging through the boggy mire
of unrelated thoughts and bad old dreams —
the ones that dig too deep. You know
the ones I mean.
The ones that steep you back in the prison
that was your life, one time.
Steep you in a jail of fears
that all your screams and tears
won't break to leak in light or rain.

And on the edge of sleep, you find
your screams are but a peep in the dawn —
a whisper for help, becoming a prayer:
Thank you. Thank you for the rain.

GEESE — a true story

Mimosa pods flutter to the ground in no hurry,
like summer's butterflies.
Crow bends the top of a cedar with his burly blackness
under a pale evening moon.

First rain — wild geese gather
their many voices from the music
of water falling on leaves. They gather
from the wet gray air in their widened nostrils,
from the warm drops on their slick skin
the knowledge, the urgency
to blend the many voices into choir
for the pure harmony of it.
The days and miles of distant travel live on in tribal memory.

The first voice cries like a rusty hinge on an old gate.
Others rise in a siren, warning of catastrophe somewhere, anywhere.
The calls drift over square lawns, the dog park,
the water treatment plant, the river.
The geese form a chevron in order of experience,
seniors at the front, young at the outer flanks,
where they can observe the elders.
They land on the river and disperse.

Two girls are floating in red plastic kayaks
into a cluster of geese. Deliberately.

The geese politely part to let them pass.
These birds have seen everything on the river,
from jet boats to plastic swimming pools
and barking dogs. The girls float into the flock
again, swatting paddles at the geese.

An odious cry explodes from the cluster.
In a matter of seconds, an entire chevron
from out of the gray descends on the girls.
They scream and wave paddles. Seriously.
And another chevron from out of another gray
arrives on the scene, sounding like
a team of emergency vehicles. Then another,
and another. The girls are unhurt and terrified.

We all learned one more thing about the world
that evening.

GRANDMA TELLER

I see her at the Navajo Indian fair
curled up in her wheel-chair —
a ball of pain and age, trying
to be comfortable in her present form.
Her chin is inches from her knees,
her out-stretched hands spin like spiders.

She speaks only Navajo these days.
Near the end of her life, she is attaining
the Spider nature, resembling more and more
Spider Woman, the grandmother of all weavers.
Full of the wisdom needed to abide old age,
and committed to the world she is in.

She can still turn a sheep-full of wool
into fine yarn in one afternoon.

part two

THREADS

The threads of my thought weave
in and out through the fabric of this life
as a person on earth, with a mind
created by a clumsy seamstress —
stitches inappropriately long
connecting
in multiple dimensions
back and forth through time
and place and perception
connecting neurons in a brain —
the superhighways with off-ramps
to cities long forgotten.

MY DESK

I remember sitting under it during my "nap time," before I was three.
My father used it as a desk.
My mother used it as a sewing table.
It lived in their bedroom, where I took
my daily "naps."
I always felt in my own world then.
I entered the toddler territory of
out-of-sight, out-of-mind.
I could do anything.

Once I crawled under the desk and
found the scissors.
Wondering what could be done with them
I tried them out on the black
sewing machine cord.
Just as Mom entered the room,
something big happened on the cord.
Something big happened at the door.

I didn't know which was most important,
but I assumed it was my mother.
So I don't remember seeing the spark.

I inherited my desk from my father.
Like him, it has seen the worst of me.
Once during "nap time"
I had to poop. I knew I had to "nap"
until Mom opened the door.
It presented a tough dilemma.
I had recently been potty-trained, so
I decided to poop on the floor.
When she finally opened the door
her distress confused me.

The space under the desk
comforted me.

ONE OLD LADY'S FIX FOR THE DAY GRAVITY HOLDS YOU LIKE A STRAITJACKET

A good latte, and if you're lucky like me,
someone to bring it too you.
Open all the window-shades.
Stare out the window into the
                          Oregon Grape waving
bright yellow in the wind.

Walk around the house once or twice
while staring into your head
        or heart.
Enjoy one hit of mild weed.
Take two tylenol.
Use your inhaler.

Put on music
that makes you want to dance.
Dance
with music filling your ears,
the beat filling your legs,
the trees and river out the window
filling your eyes.
Walk away from your phone
outside, into the weeds.

Then take a nap.

DIGGING

I dig the dirt not in sunshine
but under the soft April gray.
I have done it many times before
and, flesh forbid, may do it again.
In any event, cottonwood fluff
fills the air like snow.
Furry black bumblebees hover
over yellow blossoms of Oregon Grape.
White flowers on plums, apples, and
wild alyssum will be back next year.
A raccoon will build her nest under
our house, having already harvested
the floor insulation to line it.

And the familiar smells will welcome
the ones stuck in the nadir
of gray air and sluggish neurons.
I mean the chickadees, the old women,
children who know only their feelings
and aren't yet aware of cycles.

SEASON OF FRAGRANCE AND MUSIC

Walking among the blooming lilacs,
a longing takes hold in my chest.
I am already missing them, knowing
that they won't last long. And yet
they are more permanent than I.

Perennialism is a property of roots
that don't move much, but
have a deep connection to the earth;
of this river and its music of splash
and resistance to rocks.

Newly hatched yellow goslings
float beside their parents, who
protect them well.
Geese chatter all day long,
probably sending important messages.
They must know that all their
little yellow puffballs won't survive.
But they try hard and are
formidable guards of each other.
The have a culture of migration which
requires cooperation for success.

I find it difficult to imagine such an effort
in my own culture.
Athletics is the only model
that comes to mind. Or maybe the military.
You follow your leader
and hold your assigned position.
I find it beautiful among the geese.

CATALINA HILLS

I come here for the birds, the sunshine
and the warm colored mountains, almost bare.
Mourning doves cry across the landscape,
defining evenings in the pink canyons.

Today, a new bird song seems to soar
from the bottom of its scale to the top,
out of the human range and into
the clear blue of morning. I wonder
if there are more scales
up there beyond thin clouds?
A new and exciting music,
if only we could hear it?

Of course, someone up in Silicon Valley
figured part of it out decades ago.
Digital eardrums, or some such thing.

But this is an old, old music — too old
for us to understand. Digital eardrums
only parse the sounds.
The music must come from long ago, from
the prehistoric time when Bird and Mammal
evolved in different lines on the Tree,
already full of song.

Or is music older than life?
Did it all begin, not with the Word,
but with the Music?

FEELINGS

She doesn't like the way she feels.
She was lifted onto the plane
from a wheelchair, accompanied by
a man and a small, alert but
well-behaved dog. A comfort companion.
In addition to her presumed husband.
The companion may have been for him.

"I don't like the way I feel, Sammy."
"Okay."
Probably in their eighties, I thought.
Ten years older than me.
Her accent was New Yorkish.

"I'm glad my woiking days ah oveh.
I can hahdly keep my ayes open!"

I may be younger, but I understand.

"I'm hungry, Sammy. Ah we going to a
restaurant?"
"Yes."
"I hope I don't fohget my cane, Sammy."
"I'll remember."

"I don't like the way I feel, Sammy."

What pills does she take to stay alive?
Does he give them to her?
And what to make her feel better?
She still doesn't like the way she feels.
Neither do I. Sammy probably doesn't
either. Even though we can still walk, carry our luggage, and think
clearly.
Except when I don't.

30

Huila, the Yaqui doctor created by Luis Urrea, says feelings are not
real — not
part of the Universe. They are only yours.
Ignore them.

Old age is not about feeling good, folks,
despite what we see in television ads
featuring old people who take Lyrica
and play ball with their grandchildren.

When did she last enjoy making love?
Does she wonder how he feels?

"I'm hungry, Sammy. Ah we going to a
restaurant?"
"Yes."
"Well what's holding us up?"
"I don't know. We're on an airplane."

MY FIRST

When you were born, I was afraid of you.
So tiny, so pale, chest heaving so hard
yet taking in the air.
Afraid for you, implying impossible loss.
It was my love that I feared.
Two pounds eleven ounces in 1970.
You got tired of breathing. It was so hard.
The nurses gave you oxygen, the
universe's newest gas.
They were hopeful. I couldn't hold you
for all the tubes feeding you
what I could not. Not be
a proper mother.
Two months of watching.
My milk dried up.
The baby in the neighboring incubator
died. His name was Jesse.
I finally brought you home, beautiful.
Red hair sticking out from your head
like Sputnik, because it had been shaved.
Wonderous bright brown eyes
full of intelligence about survival.

Yet all the people could say was, "She is
so tiny!"

CROOKED PINE

Lithe, barely-clad bodies
 dance in the dust, shaking
what there is to shake, one
exposing a snail tatoo.
Those who have given up on walking
tap a foot on the floor
of a motor-chair. And those
who still try, backs arched over a cane,
jiggle to a rhythm
not coming from the stage.

Fiddler tells a joke about using his phone
to learn how
to open a lobster. And
the festival volunteer whose beard
reached his breast only last year
has allowed it to reach his belly-button,
and now clog-dances with a brace around his knee.

All this, surrounded by Sierra
Ponderosa pines. One
broke its top some time ago.
But a side branch took over
reaching for the sun, and now
the tree is crooked.
Another is poised to fall
on the restrooms.

The woman sitting next to me
just ate a spinach salad, followed by
a whole package of Chitos.
She may be the only black person
in the crowd. Her name is Terri.

The Big Thing this year is
outrageously large ladies' hats,
feathered in the least ambiguous
of colors. One of the good dancers
is an elderly woman in a hat,
twirling hoola-hoop. She is
shorter than Me!

The blind fiddler is apparently
the best in the world. He is visiting
with a young man holding an infant
with a hare-lip. Such imperfections
don't matter to the blind. And
nobody has yet proven that
we don't all come from the stars.

FOREVER NOMAD

The Redwood forest along Mill Creek
is quiet today. The same giants
still stand, the same fallen still lie
as on my last visit.
Three years is a short time
in a Redwood's existence.
The fallen nurse new trees,
huckleberries, ferns —
an immortal society that
not even fire can extinguish.
They know me as another
creature that moves away,
always away, not content with
stillness as it abides
in this greenscape. Roots
forever uprooted move me
along toward nothing.

This visit makes my day
but it can't make tomorrow.
The roots want new ground
to touch without commitment
and move along like Mill Creek.
Always moving away, always
different water. Hominids
were born to be nomads.
Haven't yet learned
to settle down
and let life go on.

CONSPIRACY THEORY

The season of flowers has wilted early this year, seized by rage towering
in the hearts of mankind.
Drought strikes the fields like
a poisoned dart, alarming even
the most tenacious weeds.

Our aging atmosphere has needs!
Carbon dioxide suffocates hearts afraid
of an enemy crusading through vessels
made to harbor life or love, food or blood.

Flowers fall on dry hate.
Sweetness sours.
Hearts are hijacked on the open seas
by diseases of rage and fear,
and longing for the return of
what has never been here.

Veins are replaced by wires
firing like all the beloved guns.

Yet all the discouraged suns
still burn to bring the flowers back.

WRITING ON THE RIVER

My words float in bubbles of foam
at the bottom of the riffle.
Or are they my words? They
may belong to someone else.
They have moved on downstream
anyway. But now
another cluster forms. Foam bubbles
whiten before they burst, the words
becoming something else.

A song woven by winds
in the locusts and cottonwoods
maybe.
Or the rush of the riffle itself.
And then there is the whistle
of the Tannenger before it crosses
to meet its mate.
And the cry of a lonely daughter.

Not my words, but I will claim them.

MONARCHS

Golden eggs shine like hope
on the milkweed stems.
My battle with Monsanto
is going well.
I watch through a magnifying glass
for the promised transformation.
The change is subtle.
Yet they always bloom out
 like orange flowers
 in the August sky.

This is thousands of miles
from their homeland. Yet
the monarchs of the air
stand a good chance against
the monarchs of industry.
And they are honest enough
to mate before our eyes.

part three

YELLOWJACKET SISTER

I am descended from a yellowjacket sister
who once hid fire from the animal people
high on a snowy mountain. Peaks
white with beauty and love could not
take form in this world but for me,
gnawing blood at the nadir.

Alone, I know no comfort,
        find no peace: my fire was stolen
for the beautiful people, long ago.
It has no warmth or light
        without me to weep
                in this cold black hole.

But for my stench of rotting meat,
blossoms that light the woods
could not send fragrance through the grass.
Pleasures of lovers in the sun
        could not burst into thunder
                without my hidden sting.
Song of orioles would stick to oak leaves
but for my ugly hum in decaying wood.

The kiss would turn to ice,
        caress to bloody wound,
the gift to poison knife
without my persistent
cold black pain.

HUMMINGBIRD AT THE FEEDER

She comes faithfully,
 not drawn by the shiny green glass —
reflection of grass, trees, light —
but by the bright red tip, clashing
like a stoplight against its surroundings.
Slender beak half her length
wings beating with a strength
impossible for her size,
she eyes the glass, seems not in a hurry,
belying the fury of her wings.

At times, as if in foreplay
she turns to splay herself before the window.
I feel she looks at me
          but sees something else.
Then turns again, lowers her quivering body
allowing beak to penetrate bead-hole
in the red nipple.
A tiny bead of moisture appears
on the tip of her beak. A bigger bubble
rises inside the glass.

She's off in a quantum leap to a nest
I will never see, full of children .

IN MEMORY OF MY MOTHER

We didn't hear the beginning of chirping.
We weren't prepared to listen.
I always miss the first whisper of dawn.
It's gone to the song of motors and crows
while I still sleep.

And so it was I failed to hear
the first cry of geese
that December morning.
Noticed only when the sky
was dark with warning wings
and the dirge of their deeper voice.

Although I longed to know
the beginning of snow on Preston Peak
I came too late.
Already her serpentine hair had gone white,
her fingers turned to ice.

SQUIRRELS

My father loved birds.
He was an outdoor boy all his life,
from dusty Texas farms
to the suburban house where he died.
There, he put four bird feeders for
different kinds of birds
on his back deck where tall trees
already attracted them.
Squirrels hung out there for the same reasons.
They tipped over the feeders and ate the food.
Dad said, "I don't do squirrels," and
got out his rifle.

He had been doing this all his life —
shooting squirrels, prairie dogs, rabbits.
He also served in the army, and was a
good shot. He was only using BBs.
Ashland, unlike most Southern Oregon towns,
was not having a love affair with guns.

One day, he saw a squirrel limping slowly
along the road gutter, in the hot sun.
It was very thin.
Then he saw it again, thinner still.
He noticed that he himself had developed a limp.

He put his gun away in some dark closet.
He never saw the squirrel again.

AN EVENING IN THE CITY

The city takes you to the top of things
with the ease of a motorized vertical trail.
At the end, a warm room waits.
Not winded, hot or dirty,
no mosquitoes find you.

The view through large glass windows —
dark-centered clouds in a back-lit sky
is more pleasing to the eye
for the jagged interruptions of
buildings, made from the mind
of a man sitting high behind
another glass out there.

It is true that a tree on a mountain top
inspires in me a deeper sense of the ten-thousand beings
than do glass buildings.

Yet the pleasure of form in the mind
is its own sensation, like the taste of this wine.
The man behind the glass
is looking my way, trying to measure
an atom of pleasure at that point
on the gyre of my mind
where it meets the mind of clouds.

KARMA

Comfort seems not
to be born in every seed.
Not to be near
the meaning of life,
not to be a valid pursuit,
despite our founding fathers'
naive proclamation:
the one about life, liberty
          and bullshit.

Neither is it earned
by mother or child, or learned
in unconsoled baby cries.
          It defies pursuit, effort, mind
and seems to reside
in the winding helix
of no direction but time.

PAIN

Limbs rage red against the sunset,
their angry cells cry in birdsong.
Before long, stars will cool the sky,
the raging will hide in the silence of veins.
Leaves will breathe oxygen for a change.
Roots will try to restore cool comfort before
a waking sun begins to burn again.
And then, the sparks will ignite
the clash of pans in the kitchen,
memories in the mind.
Flames will consume
fresh leaves that reach for rain
as birdsong blows away with the clouds.

LANGUAGE

Our brave leaders are saying,
as they did after Sputnik
that we must learn foreign tongues.
Then we would understand the plots
we could hear about on Al Jazeer,
and catch the Chinese stealing designs
for our widgets: a tough assignment
for Americans who say, "YOU know"
instead of what we really mean.

The slang of underclass and teens
serves to hide subculture from mainstream.
(The phone conversations of my son
could have been in foreign tongues!)
The rapper's eloquent abuse
may have its own clandestine use.

And just listen to the Orioles!
They seem to own the airwaves in May,
exclaiming above grinding machines
in intricate tones of mysterious meaning.
THEY have adapted their tones
to be heard among cell phones!

I must admit that I wonder more
about Oriole than Arabic.
I would learn it if I could
simply out of respect
for others in my neighborhood.

MEDITATION

Air of eons enters, one breath at a time,
raising the belly, moving the dust of memory,
bringing in its place new blossoms.

The second breath carries an offering:
fresh dew of morning leaves
to quench the goddess' tongue
where a song is budding.

With the third a breeze of jasmine
whispers white among its leaves,
eases the burden of smoke.

The four breath rides on a trill,
an oriole singing in July;
hope replenishes, the melody
blooms magenta.

Number five sends red petals to
her blood, where roses
       spread a feast.

With six, the wind sweeps in
filling her with emptiness again
in less than a minute.

STARS

The dream was the usual chaos of night.
Stars entered my room through closed windows
becoming people I used to know.
They all want something from me,
crowd around me, even on the bed!

I want nothing of them, resent their trickery,
entering as stars. I push
as they edge closer, refusing to join the
constellation.
It was not of my making!

I push and shout, "Get out, Get out!"

As dawn intrudes through my eyelids
that voice is lost in s song
among the morning birds.

NAMING THE TREES

The mountain opens its mouth to speak.
No one but the wind is listening.
Guide books and maps open,
the tourists talk about
which mountain to climb and
where to eat breakfast. The mountain
closes, refusing to tell them anything.
Talks to the wind instead. No one
is listening other than an owner who
charges twenty-eight dollars
for breakfast.

Trees whisper and wave. The people
call them "beautiful." They don't
hear the whisper. Want to name the
nameless trees. They want to find
the nameless mountain on the map.
As if to name is to own in some way.
Nothing reveals its real name, Each one
must find their own true name
and hold it in their hearts .

The wind moves the tree
in a nameless dance, his mouth
on her ear. She hears her own name.
Her arm moves down his body
but he is gone. Her longing swells
beneath seed-laden branches,
drops down into her roots,
into the ground,
and she is free.

RAPTURE

They stood around the departure pad —
      white on the desert sand —
that promised them another chance
      in an undiscovered land.
In tight concentric circles
they gathered around the pad
silent, still, but for the crunch
on the weak, the poor, the sad:
souls who were as yet unsaved,
unwealthy, out of line,
who had no faith in Capital
or Intelligent Design.

They began the ascent by standing on top
of the bodies of those Marked beasts,
their voices roaring a warning
of the Rapture and upcoming feast
when the Haves, the Have-mores, the Base
pick the beasties clean
leaving only their own Blessed race
and some beasties to tend their machines.
They waited and listened for the sound
they fully expected to hear:
Angel Voices encoded within
the rocket's roaring take-off gear.

But then the ground began to rise.
The beasties came to their feet.
The Blessed race was so surprised
it forgot it was elite
and crawled on its belly to regain
its place at the head of the line
leading to the Sacred Pad
which would join them with the Divine.

Meanwhile, the Beasties were hearing a song
which inspired them so to rise —
a song the blessed race couldn't hear,
and that led to its demise.
As the Newly Risen approached the Pad,
they saw it was a field of Corn
where Spider Grandmother sang like mad
to grow a stalk before the morn
tall enough to take her brood
of simple-living animal kin
up to the hole leading to a New World
where they had a chance to begin again.

And still, the blessed crawled and listened
for the sound they fully expected to hear:
angel voices encoded within
the rocket's roaring take-off gear.
They didn't hear the Beastie voices
joining Spider Grandmother's song
or see the growing stalk of Corn
that would pierce the New World before long.

The Fifth World had been a promise expressed
in the Bible, Native Myth and Koran
but none of the animals, beast or blest,
had followed through with the Sacred Plan.
Instead of tending the tender land,
they poisoned it, robbed it, washed it away —
without any offering, turned it to sand —
the sand they were standing on today.
Instead of blessing the needy, the meek,
they stole from them, themselves to bless
with mansions, towers, SUV's,
the making of which left a terrible mess,

poisoning beasties who made the stuff
or lived too near the operations.
They left the clean-up of the duff
to future beastie generations.
They forgot that the covenant with their god
included the land with its microbes and beasts —
they broke it apart, rode it rough-shod
in order to finish their fattening feast.

And finished it was, for by the morn
their god's web was broken and twisted awry,
and Spider Grandmother's stalk of Corn
had pierced the Portal in the sky.
She was sufficiently wise and bold
to mend the dreadful situation,
so around the stalk she spun with gold
another Story of Creation.
As she worked the Beasties climbed
and sang behind her as she spun
and the journey upward took such a long time
that they spoke the same language before they were done.

When they reached the top, she said to Mole,
"Go ye forth underground and find
what dangers await us above this hole
before we leave it behind."
She sat on his ear to give him advise
as he plowed their way through the earth,
and what he learned right away wasn't nice,
and he whispered softly to her:
"The only danger lies with our folk,
the human kind in the clan.
I'd hate to knock them off the stalk,
so we need to come up with a plan.
Perhaps, Grandma, you could give them a duty —

something no one else can do
with their reading and writing and chattering hooty
so they don't have time for their deep doo-doo."

"That's easy!" to Mole she cheerfully said.
"I need someone to keep the new Tale
I've woven in gold within our Web,
for my memory is old and frail."
"That's a job that will keep them busy," said Mole
as they made their way back to the stalk
and invited all creatures out of the hole
to hear Spider Grandmother talk:

"This Gold is a story we must hold
together even when we are far apart.
Not a thread can be broken or sold
for each is the life-blood to someone's heart.
And as the other five worlds have told,
nothing of value can replace the Gold.

So — Human Beasties, I give to you
the Sacred duty to keep it alive.
Since you travel farther than most of us do,
you can insure that the Story survives.
Now — Birds, go forth and remember your song.
Procreate so your race is strong.
Fish, keep the Waters alive and clean
and procreate into every stream.
Bugs, go forth and polinate
and don't forget to procreate.
All you four-leggeds, find your place
where each of you can expand your race.
Man, spread the Tale with imagination
but PLEASE, control your procreation.

(In reference to the mythology of Pueblo Peoples and their heroine,
Spider Grandmother, who solves human problems.)

part four

GREEN SEA TURTLE

Turtle in the green clear brine,
my eyes stare long into the water
in order to separate you from the rocks.
You are old! Old enough
to remember friendlier times.
The lines upon your shell
tell the epic:
designs dreamed by the old gods,
before they were thrown
into the mountain's fire.
And the turtle remembers.

Newer gods did not
paint crosses on the turtle's back.
They did not deem the creature
worthy of Art.

The old folks say:
When the Water finally met the Land,
crawling things were born.
Turtle. Honu.
A new creation on a new
earthly place.
And he survives,
alive through all the many worlds of men.

STILL

Still the choir of birds calls in from the cactus.
The mountains press against a starry sky.
You are still a part of the picture,
as a golden sunset sings goodbye.

I see you in the silver raindrops falling,
and in golden leaves floating down the stream —
among the loved ones gone before you.
We're all in the falling drops of rain.

AUNT LEONA

She held out her hand, blue veins rising above the bones.
"Could you help me? It's not that I can't walk.
I just can't see the ground!"
Distorted old eyes, watery blue, smiled behind thick glass.
Her wrinkled hand grasped my arm
and warmed against my summer skin.

Only ninety-three years since she arrived too soon
out of a young mother's womb, a
skinny frightening thing, wiggling pinkish-blue,
limbs the size of her father's fingers.

He put her in a shoe-box, set it on the edge
of a wood-fired oven;
Rode the horse fourteen miles
to get the country doctor.
Tried to find a mid-wife on the way.
No luck.
The young mother tended her own first birth.
Found an eye-dropper, some sugar. Warmed water
on the stove beside the babe — still alive,
tiny chest heaving in the air. Two-and-a-half pounds
all labored to bring in the air of her new world.

And she did bring it in; did the one thing
the others couldn't do. And she did
see the ground and walk it for ninety years.
No disease ever found her.
Then one morning at one-hundred-and-one
she was found healthy, but dead.

A FATHER

He was smaller today than she'd seen him before.
Said he now walks with a stoop
even when nothing hurts.
Though his eyes are still alert
he misses bits of conversation.
Yet he finds ways to gracefully be
a part of things.
Rather than talk to the children much
he absorbs their ambience and
basks in their presence.

He walks with them through
the jungle to the creek, though rocks
threaten to trip his feet.
He listens with her to the birds,
laughs at the children swimming.

It seems that anger has
entirely vanished from his heart
and his countenance.
So why does she still fear him?

He once told her that he has a "mean streak"
and she believed him.
Is it that which she still fears
streaking down her spine from time to time?

IN THE SKY

In the sky, a silver plane reflects the sun like a daytime star;
trails a long sooty cloud that can write words, in the sky.
It is a thing not alive, yet moves like a hawk.
Just as a human body harbors smaller beings —
like microbes and viruses —
this silver plane contains over a hundred entire persons.
They're hungry. They awoke
very early in the morning to catch the plane,
and didn't eat; but the plane was stubborn.
They all had to sit on board for three hours
while it got into a better mood.

Recently, due to foolish business practices,
airplanes have stopped serving food on short flights;
short for the airplane.
Not short for starving, anxious people with backaches.
Unlike human microbes,
they couldn't eat the plane. They weren't true omnivores
after all.

The silver hawk speaks in the low rumble of engine-speak
just to remind you that it is not a living thing, like a corporation.
It is incapable of sympathy,
much like a corporation.
When it is told by higher powers
to land on the ground, it has a fit and screams,
which really annoys the hungry passengers.
It likes to fly
in the sky.

KAPOHO BAY, HAWAII

I am trying to separate the turtles from the rocks,
trying to see their exact contours,
amidst the larger pattern of rock puzzles —
like the cell structures of human skin, or
turtle skin. Earth skin.
New skin, sculpted by the goddess Pele,
as the old story goes.

Is there a way to begin again?
Is there a way to be good again?
The question deserves many hours
of staring into the water
separating the turtles from the rocks.

The warm places in the water
as I swim
seem to say that Pele is
giving birth again, despite
her many disappointments.
It is her life.

LLAPINGACHOS

I am at this time another animal crawling
on a small part of the earth —
another two-legged
with a bad back, crawling through the dirt,
reaching down to drag out potatoes:
big and red, small and blue —
another miracle of the soil.

Now earthworms crawl with me.
There were none under the grass
that grew here two years ago.
They came for the cool
dampness of dead leaves
that I spread to kill this part
of a too-big suburban lawn.
Potatoes took over.
What is grass to us?

I read in an old history
that potatoes and cheese make
a nutritionally complete diet.
Above the fragrance of fertile earth
rises the steamy pungency of llapingachos.

MY TWIN GRANDSONS

They came into the light too soon,
their tiny lungs unready
for the air of this world.
Toxemia.
Nothing else to do
but die or birth,
mother and two tender boys.

Nothing else to do but
employ the tubes, concoctions
care
of modern medicine;
Minuscule veins
tapped open to the hope
of surfactant and other magic names.
You would think there wouldn't have been room.
But there is always more of things than we think.

They were miniature forms of perfect men,
legs the size of fingers,
fingers lacy bluish threads,
always moving.

And though we were surrounded by tears,
I always knew I would see them running,
pointing, shouting "Dog!"

PURPLE FINCH

Oh Purple Finch, you are the perfect bird!
Your voice pure poetry without words —
the song you sing in the Palo Verde tree
a prelude to all languages, in a melody
unheard until you came along.

When your family gathers above the feeders,
the music of your chorus is about love.
What else could bring such longing to my heart?

I long to stroke the soft feathers along your back,
those heavenly structures that part your hair
so perfectly, paint you in unearthly colors — not purple,
and take you into the fragrant air.
They define your own perfection,
announcing a beauty that is complete.

BIRDS AT THE LIZARD ROCK HOUSE

The doves and the quail, the squirrels and sparrows here
may have surpassed human beings
in their ability to tolerate one another.
They eat at the same cafeteria —
the one of rocks splattered with seed
falling from the feeder above.
They peck and scratch in little circles, side by side in spontaneous dance,
each wearing a different dress.

Their subtle colors ripple over
rough pink rocks
like a stream on a cloudy day.
Fabrics in designs
woven long ago by the gods
melt together over the ground.

Quail wears soft rufus hair
under a black antenna, coiled,
as though it could spring upward
to touch the Palo Verde branches.
Black spots on the dove's back
flow into the sparrow's mocha-
with-chocolate-syrup feathers.
Finches almost touch the sparrows
at the feeder. The birds speak
all at once, in their different tongues.
Meanwhile, people slaughter their own kind
across the world.

FOOD CHAIN

Oh, Bluejay, you thought you were lucky.
You stole an egg from Robin, that pretty bird,
but here on the dusty ground
by the blackberries sweet and full,
I found only your feathers
scattered over pale blue shells.
Hawk was luckier than you.
He stole your egg and your meat.
He chuckles, fat, in the seat of the pine.
But, oh, Bluejay, I see that your diet
was unhealthy — too many dog kibbles and
french fries left in parking lots laced with
motor oil.
Now Hawk's wife can't lay a decent egg.
They have no shell, they look like jelly.
He wasn't as lucky as he thought.
As for your wife, she didn't mourn for long.
She's laying someone else's eggs
and they are strong.

SHOES

His shoes live wherever they please
now
in the house, tripping my
failing eyes.

Wherever I go they stop me,
and I am no longer annoyed,
I wish they were on his feet.

They are now my only
companions in the evenings,
telling me their stories,
which I've heard before
and now love more than I did back then.

REPURPOSING MY MOTHER'S WOOL

She fell in love with wool
during the last years of her life.
Sheared it off a sheep named Angela,
picked and combed out the burrs and sticks
and brambles that Angela collected
as she rambled the fence around her pasture.
Love for the smell of a sheep's shorn coat,
for the sticky feel of lanolin, is acquired
through a vision of the soft scarf in
natural colors — the dull green of moss,
brown bark of oak, silky
long white fiber of angora goat,
oily dark brown dreads and clumps
of clean white sheep hair,
looking like an angel.

The smell and touch of it
overwhelmed her senses
with warm connections: sheep
in cumulous clouds
resting on spring grasses,
smelling the earth, transforming
the lean grass into greasy lanolin
and soft curls in shades
white to the darkest brown
the earth has to offer. It spins
into fine yarn, atomic attraction causing
hairs to line up and cling to one another.
Weaving it all together is satisfying as
creating a universe.

And here I am, twenty-six years after her death,
my hands fondling the stuff, joining her
in the vision.
It is unspinnable, the spinners told me.
It is too old.

I have done with it what I could —
made a stuffed sheep for my grandson,
(oh, she would have loved that),
worked bits of it into my weavings
on her loom, the Gilmore.
Stuffed old socks with it for
winter pipe insulation. (THAT might have
made her cry.)

And now it is autumn. The artichokes need
protection from frost. So do the strawberries.
My hands in the thick warm hair feel so protected
they seem to be sleeping.
When they awake, I know what they will do.

They will fulfill another vision and
return what was once alive — and feels to be still —
to the lean grasses where the stuff began.

SOLDIERS

Waves line up against the shore, uniform
like soldiers awaiting turns
for refuge in the sand; each
a story of battle, herding
like cattle on a gory sea.

They seek refuge in the land
that is supposed to taste so good;
they form a still-life in motion
on an ocean of change,
where each speck of foam
makes a world of its own.

And yet,
        they keep drifting back to sea,
can't ever seem to get home;
can never again taste the land
that should be so good.
Their mouths are full of salt and sand.
Their dreams are full of blood.

SURVIVORS

Suddenly the honey-bees were gone from the hives.
No bodies were found — anywhere.
Yet the April woods sound of humming.
Smell of pollen. And you can find the furry survivors
hiding in blossoms, no matter how tiny,
secretly feasting.

And on the desert! How did they know
there would be flowers?

After the massacre by poison and disease,
starvation by sugar-water,
the ragged remnants of tribes must have fled
to remote fringes of the world.
No one knew. They were thought dead.
It was not a rich life, but better than slavery.

And those hives were slave ships —
boxes stacked high in foreign fields
like Spanish missions on the desert.

Those orchards were tempting, of course,
with endless billows of creamy pink blossoms.
Tempting like the stories of Jesus and the santos.
But invisible poisons
laced those graceful pink skirts.
The disease-infested vestments clothed
a treachery which few survived.
It tore the delicate weave of a fabric
spun over generations.

The stories of the orchards were about money,
not bees nor honey, nor
the internal spinning and humming of a hive.
Not about peaches dripping
the soothing sweet juice of full ripening.
Those stories were about fruit to pick green,
bland as the landscape,
packed into boxes, stacked onto trucks.
They wove a fabric of highways to
certain destinations, and not others.
Stories about Some, and not Others.

Survivors reside on the edges, in shadows,
by rushing monkey-flower streams,
in the back row of churches
where tears can be shed, unseen:
in the weeds and dust on the outskirts of town,
where escape is easy.

THE DIVORCE

The bank account is amiably divided,
and the children, too,
luckily even in number.
The grass is awarded to me,
with chunks of rotten wood
falling from our house.
You may have the cars —
they are too much trouble.

Now we have finally come to agree.
The unsettled autumn air
thrashes the last of my passion
into lustful clinging
to this pile of yellow leaves,
to these walls, and this chair.

The quicksand awarded to me,
as you drive away with
a part of me so young
you never knew it.

THE GREAT WHITE LANDLORD 1/17

A tower is not born from the land.
It steals its parts from far-away places.
From you and me, and the natives, and
the Mother in all of us.
As its erection grows, the Few are invited in
to the swelling capillaries.
Its pleasure is in the growing, not
in any way the giving.

The many are left on the ground floor
with no ground.

The Mother is milked
like the Holstein cow
in a filthy barn of Commerce.
When that cow is milked dry
the Landlord moves on to another cow, until
one day, all the cows collapse into
a heap of dry bones.
The tower, without the pleasure of love,
shrinks into a withered old man.

STORIES

I'm watching the whitecaps bounce down the river.
Stories sail through my brain like the whispy white clouds
sailing across the sky, telling themselves
over and over: as though they have their own lives and want to be
remembered.
The one about a grandfather I never met, and still don't know why he
disappeared.
And the traumatic birth of my first child.
My mother had one about a couple whom
she suspected of having sex with their clothes on.

Over and over, always the same.

Then my other grandfather's story,
about a "colored woman" in front of him who told the store clerk,
"I only have a nickel and some small change."
Oh, and then my own, mostly excuses for being what I am.
But my father's were the best,
at least the first time I heard them.
Are his ashes, recently scattered upon this very river, still telling me their
stories? I can't help hearing them.
Suddenly my unseeing eyes return
to this moment, to this very river.
Osprey dives for fish. Catches it. Buzzard is not far behind.

part five

ROCKS AND THOUGHTS

Little rocks on the beach today
       so clean:
whites pure, and serpentine
green, bright
under a gray ocean sky
right next to a sombre sea.
They sparkle like clear thoughts
just emerging from a murky mind;
like jewels just dug out of the rough,
spread out before the morning,
mourning world.
Thoughts of bloated bodies,
fathers and mothers sucked in by the sea
an ocean away, on a stage before
the daughters and sons
who can never forget.

Shining stones beg us to
remember with them
the unbirthing of that December.

Some could be thoughts of my own
if I chose to make a claim. But
should I take them home,
they are sure to lose the light that is born
in the sharing under an ocean sky.

(RE: THE TSUNAMI OF 2007)

LAUREY

She was low as the belly of a snake,
as if she didn't know that
the cancer would take him soon.
One who loves loses tears from
deep within Earth's well.
They left her withered and thin —
a blade of autumn grass in spring.

She had studied his I.V. bottles,
oxygen, blood, and knew
but now that he was gone,
freedom eluded her
just like the spring.

Then the Indian Doctor came
and sang a song —
       Do you hear the wind
       of the Raven's wing,
the great heart beating in the sky?
It's the breath traveling through everything.
It's your love singing on the other side.
Made a sacred tea from the well
to feed her body with lost tears. Lay
cedar bows at the door where spirits dwell.
Made a bath from sacred plants
where the patient lay for a day,

Then dried her body and her tears
and went out to see the Raven fly away.

MIRROR

The glass above the bathroom sink
these sixty years
 used to scare me
when I went to pee at night.
She showed me unfamiliar forms
that I could not face so
I tried to terrorize them with the light.

Then she gained my trust one year,
thrust me under her power, made me
a minion of her fickle opinions.
I tried to be her friend, said words of love
 that stuck in the air between us like
frightened spiders hanging from
threads of web.

Since my eyes began to fail
the spiders have woven a veil of
respect across the glass,
and live in the middle like
godesses.

STRANGE BUTTERFLIES

Strange butterflies in the garden this
sixtieth year of life. Long-haired
tiny sages exploring details of the earth.
White manes shine down their spines
on top of black on top of
         deep, rusty orange —
the color I imagine of hot rock
         deep within.
Layered colors, like slices of ancient earth
         or parfait.
Those long white hairs along the spine
remind me of nerves seeking pleasure
as they brush the air. I imagine
orgasm in their ripples.

So many feet touch on invisible treasures
found only in this ground, hear
the early sounds of earth and
whispering microbes.

After we tilled, they set up camp in a weedy corner.
The weeds will stay there, in their honor.

Strange butterflies are here as well this year —
chocolate with white fringe around the wings.
They hover around flowers and manure.

Are these two really one being?
Am I seeing my daughter and
her baby self at once, as
I have so often dreamed?

MAY

Evenings are green in the woods out the window
where rain has scrubbed away at ever leaf
every day for a month.
Just when we thought we had seen
the outer limits of green, shining in
streaks of light through the trees,
some cloud lets loose again, cleaning
everything away, everything that could
stop the pure essence — Absolute Green —
could stop it from screaming out of the earth,
up the roots and out the leaves
dazzeling jewels before out hungry eyes.

I want to hold this emerald dream until
the hot dust of August weighs on branches
like the burden of memory.

GRAY SQUIRRELS

After seeing foxes every day
I see how much alike you are
and wonder if you are related
somehow, outside of taxonomy.
The tail tells it all,
its shimmering silver falling on a plume,
arched like a quarter-moon.
Across the ground it bounces
like a being all its own.
The small round ball of your body
quietly sniffs the grass, watches the dog.
In the trees, your chattering
reminds me of monkeys in a jungle.
With your friends you transform conifers,
make me smell rotting fruit around their roots,
see bright birds among their limbs.

You are no common rodent
stealing garlic from the garden.
You are a chameleon king bringing
cinnamon and myhrr to our manger.
You're in my tunes, pulling out the notes,
the rhythm, joy, effort of my fingers
on your back, running. Pulling the lines
 along by your side, out of my own mind,
into the flowers for sharing.
 You pull my self up the tree
so it can see from your eyes,
nose, ears, feet, tongue licking pitch
off the cones. mmmmmm!

RAIN

Rain on the roof sounds like lizards
pattering in the wall. It rises
to crescendo, plopping, pounding
the gutter. A jagged rhythm like
foreign jazz, racing on a mountain road.
The garden earth drinks it all, can
dance to any beat. My heart leaps
and falls, tripping over its feet.
Lizards in the wall go still
as if to a lullaby.

A universe of drops fall
like sand grains on a beach —
in rain they come,
striking out of time, each drop
a universe of its own
and yet we call it Rain.

HUNTING MIND

The lizard lies still as stone
on the cement patio,
his head in the shadow,
tail in the sun —
still as death for as long
as I can sit watching.

It ignores a parade of tiny black ants
which exude the odor of cloying perfume.
It agrees with me on that.
Yet it is in the hunting mind.

And so am I, hunting comfort
in the frail afternoon.
I think my mind is big.
I can afford to wonder about a lizard
for awhile.
Even though I won't be eating it.

But soon I will be hunting for a beer, and
something else, for dinner.
When I was young, I hunted for 'fun' —
something more than ordinary evenings.

Enlightenment is said to be
freedom from desire.
Its rarity is proof of the power
of the hunting mind,
which I still share with the lizard.

PRAISE THE IMPORTANT THINGS

Sing praises of Lizard
lying perfectly still on vertical foundation blocks.
A silent hunter, who is not a pest,
and so is unafraid.
She seeks shade now, sun then,
and particular bugs who suit her taste.

Sing praises to cool grass
under madrone and fir this July day,
and to River not far away
who feeds Lizard with the insect world,
and us with her cool and perfectly clear
liquid jewel.

I sing your praises as you arrange
the barbecue fire perfectly around
your round black water pot,
pipe in the side of your mouth,
your fingers setting each briquet
square in its place.

Sing praises to the shadows
protecting murmurs and secrets
outside our field of vision.

Sing praises to the evening
as it evens out the pulses of the day,
and like a bridge in a song
clears the way for peace in the night.

CHICKADEES

All day this first of May
the high cry of chickadees
slices through clouds
      hesitant to burst;
cuts through the rumble of
thunder on the mountain;
pierces small holes for moonbeams
in the drone of thought.

DAY'S END

I cherish the ends of the days,
when body dies down with the light
and imagination explores
the darkening outdoors
one last time before sleep.
No challenges await, and the self
that feels accomplishment and pain
scatters among raindrops dripping off leaves.

BIRTH

One October night,
wind-breath softly stirring treetops,
full Moon sings behind a cloud.

His rainbow rings send down his song
and glowing heavens draw me out
of a sphere within spheres,
hatching from an egg within an egg
within an egg, waking
dreams into more dreams.

I wonder when I will finally awake
and if I will ever be born.

STRIPPING

First went the hair, after
so many years, combed, curled,
braided, groomed. Went to
sick children who lost it too soon.
I wish it had power, could stop
their suffering.

Next the eyes, so tired of crying,
no longer good at seeing through
glass or air, words or love.
Went to Coyote,
who is always losing his own.

And then the words themselves,
too worn to wear again,
sent to clouds to fall as rain
somewhere, in another time.

Now it's sadly come to pass
that tingling in the spine,
      Pleasure Absolute,
must find a sturdier shrine
to carry on her beauty.
I think I hear her humming
      in a sunflower.

And so there remains a mind,
no good alone but perhaps
if entwined in the fabric of grass,
or rolled like water over stone
could begin again to build some bones,
or maybe something softer:
feathers, caterpillars, even moss.

part six

THE MUSIC OF WAVES

An uproar of tone and rhythm,
music of waves sloshing on the lava shore
washes through my body from the toes
and upward, like an internal massage.
My brain is rinsed clean.

I find a tiny Hawaii in the midst
of a big Pacific, and suddenly know —
absolutely — what I really am.
I stand a waving frond of palm
born in the black rock of
the newest land on earth.

THE SWARM

First came the sound — "The Word" —
so-to-speak. Some say
that's how the Universe began.

It was a mechanical sound, constant
with neither shape nor crescendos.
At a closer look — the sound
was coming from not one but
many, so tuned to a certain
frequency that
the many harmonized as one
    tiny chainsaw.
Slowly the spaces between the many
grew smaller, and the many joined
and took the form of a being
with four limbs and a head
as they crowded, coating
the branch of a plum tree.
The sloth-ish thing was
still motoring in place
fourteen hours later —
when before my eyes
blue spaces appeared.
The one came apart at every junction
like molecules of water
evaporating in a cloud.
And the cloud moved on
to a better village location
on its own locomotion.

WHEELCHAIRS

Heroes of the frozen foggy streets, I see you
every time I leave my house in a heated car.
My being reaches out to admire your strength
as you chat side by side on the sidewalks.
And I am reminded of how I hide,
like a winter seed inside my comfort —
and depression.

The blankets covering your stumps
should be woven boldly, brightly,
like a chief's blanket
announcing your spirits, your will
to take part in the world.

The pain that brought you to your chairs
must have taught you courage, or
you wouldn't dare to travel the wicked streets,
so bare, so small, next to the roaring trucks
that may not stop for you.

You must have learned to live
with smallness, and slowness —
to life without our feigned busyness.

THORNS

These mesquite and palo verde trees,
these fifty-foot cacti and a-hundred foot palms,
even the daggered agave and yucca,
do not care a drop of water about my existence.
They care even less about the many wrongs
that I have done to others and to myself,
not to mention the spiders in my vacuum bag.

But it is the wrongs that dog me.

I stand ashamed in the midst of these uncaring plants
aiming spines at me from every direction
and become just another prickly being,
always thirsty.
What the others see in me is nothing more
than another way to get their water stolen.

UP TO THE GRINDING ROOM

You can faintly hear the hum
over the sound of traffic
even as you enter town.
This is a mill town.
Wood
at every stage and of every
size and shape — piled
anywhere you look.

The top of the hill looks out
to the ocean, and down
on little yellow moving towers
pushing and pulling hunks and slices
of denuded trees, busily here and there,
like ants dragging carcasses
through the dust.

You hear the dull grind
of heavy metal moving
against itself, slapping,
clattering along with
diesel sighs and screaming saws.

But come down to the mill
if you want to earn a buck,
without much education.

Come up to the filing room and
wade through wet sawdust.
Smell how its sourness mixes
with the smell of oil on steel.
Nothing here is made of wood or
anything that soft.

The steel moves and grinds in circles —
couldn't stop if a babe got in its way.
Giant carbide butchers spin waiting
for a victim.
Not too many logs today.
Still, they spin.

And when you've earned your buck,
go back up the hill. Let your senses
mingle in the breeze. Look out
across the water and try to picture
Japan. Or at least its lumber ships.
Listen for the hollow sigh of
breaking waves. Try to cleanse.

But the diesel sigh is already in your ears.
Grinding, whining steel screaming
through the night will never let you rest.

TRAVELERS

Robins scatter thickly across the grass,
pecking in the dirt for worms driven
upward by the rain.
The black faces on Junkos
appear to have no bodies
as they peer out from bare Mimosas.

Wild geese arrange themselves
meticulously, over the river
into the shape of a V — elders near the point,
fledgelings on the flanks
where they can see the elders.

I crawl through the dark dirt
plucking unwanted plants from the garden,
with the waning sun on my back, and
we all move slowly together on
this patch of green earth,
away from the sun and into
more distant stars.
All night, our brains visit the other worlds.

We share each others' pain and curiosity and love.
I wonder if the Stellar Jay,
whom I admire every day,
thinks I am beautiful.

SUBURBAN PUEBLO

There is a quiet that flowers on the desert
around these pueblo suburbs.
Houses all the same, crowded together like puzzle pieces,
as though in agreement that
man did not evolve as an independent being:
one with great need for his own space,
with rights to property and weapons.
He is more like a coyote, with need for the tribe.

The small yards of cactus and gravel
require no water, are half walled-in with
clean adobe bricks —
the same pink rock as the landscape.
Barely separate from the wild:
the deceptively dead-looking mesquite forest
and the prickly pear.
Home to the javelina, lizard, coyote, hawk, meadowlark.

It is agreed that these things are good:
quiet, clean blue air, a soundscape
dominated by birds, a train, coyotes —
a nightscape lit only by stars.
The afternoon is static. Single atoms
reach out to get your attention
when you touch the metal door-knob.
The evening train whistles off to Mexico.
A coyote family sings back.
All day, the Phenopepla asks the question:
eeiu? eeiu?
as though there were no finality to any of it.

FRAGILITY

She was blocking the grocery aisle
with her cart and scant bent body.
She bent lower still to read
the bottom shelf — canned soup.
Her short white hair rested
like a cap on her thin head.
Her wrinkled hand lifted each can
close to her eyes, to read ingredients.
Her eyes looked hungry,
like those of a serious hunter.

I met her later at the noodles as
she carefully read each package —
colorful curly-cues, angel hair, lasagne.
Already she had become thinner.
A wide belt held her junior-size jeans
over skinny hips.
Nothing was in her cart.

I covered the vegetable section,
my basket nearly full,
and found her again
examining the meat — a
single piece of chicken.
Admiring its fine skin or
searching for microbes —
I wasn't sure. Her cart was still empty.

Mine was so full it wouldn't steer so
I went to the check-out line.
As I left I saw the wisp of her
pull up at the end of the line,
five gallon jugs of pure water in her cart:
all that her careful hungry hunting
found satisfactory.
She must have disappeared before
she reached the door,
for I never saw her leave the store.

GARDEN

Grouse in the shadows around the garden fence
make a sound like water spilling over rocks.
Artichoke buds stand up at the ends of branches
like fists on the ends of arms,
ready to march.

White flowers of peas, cilantro, daisies,
pure as a first communion veil
glisten on heads where seeds will soon be born.
Muted colors of the earth
send their light through rocks
baptized clean by rain.

My raw hands crawl like spiders
in neat round beds surrounded
by rocks that break the hoe
and dull the tiller tines.
These forms of mind, made for pleasure,
circle and twine among the weeds,
under an aching rain.

PUERTO PENASCO

Tall pelicans perch on the rocks and wait —
white heads, vertical eyes, long bill
focused out across the gulf.
Not intent, but still, modeling Patience.
We ask each other, "What should we do next?"
"Is this a good time?" "Should we stay or leave?"

Stucco buildings stand half empty
of walls or paint,
waiting for completion or demise.
The land where they sit has been sold.
The developer sits in his trailer-shack.
Waiting.

For completion of the four-lane from L.A.
So he can sell imaginary luxury condos
to the sun-seekers of the North.

Humble hawkers walk the sand all day
with their loads of vases, jewelry, blankets.
Worried.
Will they go the way of the RV parks with palapas,
dogs, ATVs,
when the luxury class moves in?
Don't worry. That freeway will never be built.
"So where shall we eat dinner?"
Manny's on the Beach? Camper?
Meanwhile the pelicans wait for their share
somewhere beneath a dazzling sunset.

SMILES

The end of a life is seldom sudden.
Threads thin
and break into loose ends
after some pretend crescendo.
An ending undeclared by ritual.

"How in the hell can the old folks tell
it ain't gonna rain no more?"
It's easy.
A persistent burden lifts from our bones.
For a while.

But then, there is this ubiquitous assumption
of Hope,
whom we must introduce to Truth.
We learn to smile
without either one.
Hoping not to lie.

But a smile is about the Present.
Hope is about an assumed Future.

Smiling through pain is not a lie.
Smiles have never been
the property of Hope.

SLEEPLESS NIGHT

A cold animal throbs in her chest
at early dawn, or midnight, when
predators lurk on the edges of sleep,
and deep in coronary vessels.

A cold animal that warns
to flee or fight against
unseen enemies, still warm
in protozoan memory,
though bones lie frozen
in vestigial tombs.

Reptilian thing squirms her brain to alertness,
though she doesn't think she fears death.
And maybe doesn't.

The Serpent itself is the
fearsome enemy.

Though sunlight comes too soon,
it invites the lizard out to warm rocks,
where it lies harmless under a clear summer sky.

COMING HOME IN SPRING

New grass of April devours the burned-off hills.
Fire-dead wood lies unattended in these acres,
left alone to the rampages of fire, rain, spring —
a soft reminder of more deserted times,
when old trees stood where now they lie
in anonymous piles —
lie waiting.

Of times when the mountains rumbled with
fire from deep within, and This was in the making!

New grass of April devours the wrinkles of time
like perfumed oils in Egyptian baths.

What sleeps beneath the velvet skin,
in mounded tombs, in molten vaults,
in wordless cries and tuneless song,
lives and lives.

It's so easy, coming home in spring.

WATER

I am looking for a way without passion,
where flowers speak for themselves,
and there is nothing one should do.

The way would be low: the way of water,
which doesn't know SHOULD, WOULD,
                    BAD, GOOD.

I want an easy way, where effort earns no respect
and lizards lie on warm rocks.
A winding way, where mind meanders after dragonflies.
And mud is acceptable.

It is the way of blind old women,
and of babies too young to see
fine lines and corners.

And when religion has worn us
to a sharp edge, and we have won
gold metals for all our pain,
may we fall in drops of rain
off the limbs of trees,
into streams and puddles,
joining the mud, the rocks, the breeze.

INCINERATOR

He had a burning barrel in the yard
between the garden and the redwood trees.
Saturday was cleaning day, and we gathered
all the useless items of our lives,
offered them up to the rusty shrine
and watched him light the fire.
It excited our young eyes.
My father was meticulous and appreciated ritual.
We were allowed to add offerings of our own
and thrilled at their sizzle and flame.
He was raised a Southern Baptist.
Having rejected faith, he
still respected punishment and fire.
Perhaps that's why he called it
the Incinerator.

We children lived in the freedom
of the redwood trees.
One Saturday morning he found our outdoor toilet,
and was puritanically appalled.
He burned it in the fire before our eyes,
used paper and all.
Being a green country girl, I still loved
the curl of smoke and flames
when I was sixteen. It was then
that he made me burn the cigarettes,
bought with money I had earned.
Snooping in my purse, he found them,
slapped them in my hand before the fire.
It was then that he quit smoking.

LAST MARCH

A cold sun pierces the morning,
cutting fine lines among the frozen trees.
New sprouts in the garden dangle upward,
drawn toward a warm promise scantly scattered,
and downward into cold certainty.

She left with a faint breath.
The inaudible ripples changed the world,
somehow — as they must.
Nothing is insignificant.

Yesterday, she said she couldn't die
quite yet because
Her frail voice trailed off into dark closets
full of useless possessions,
which she never got around to cleaning.
She couldn't admit that
someone else would have to find their uses.

.

part seven

MY SISTER THE WIND

My sister the Wind sings songs of resistance,
in her blue dress, her dark skin,
her silver snaky hair.
She moves the Air and all of your flags.

The mimosa pods rattle like castanets and
scare the squirrel up a tree.

Clouds ride through their blue ocean,
guided by the song,
whistling against the canyon walls,
whispering, "You must resist."

The dance, the song, the caress against my skin:
the voice of resistance,
my sister the wind.

TRAVELIN' ON THE BUS

Born to travel, and haven't we, brother?
A million years from Africa to
Salt Lake City —
the time it would take to dilute black to white,
or ripen white to black,
to evolve the seed in the mind of Adam
into a KNOWING:
Homo sapiens are all alike.

The Superdome looked like
the hull of a slave ship, said the Reverend.
And he was right.
There we were, and here we are.
Five hundred years.
Not yet even on the top deck.

Sister, we traveled by foot from
cotton picking to spinning machines
in Ohio, Illinois, never singing of
graves left behind, under blue grass.
Our Blues — only soothing reminders of
empty pockets, empty stomachs, empty beds.
Emptiness is just something else to share.

You can't walk away through twenty feet of water.
So there we were, and here we are.

If we're lucky enough
to catch that bus, to rise up
from the corpses, sewage,
          bullets and bludgeons,
we might end up in someone's promised land.
I hear that Utah is white as the sand on the ground
and the heavenly spire where Gabriel blows his horn.

These people say we sat on the fence
when God and Satan tried to claim the rest.
We know, Bro, that even a barbed wire fence
is an easy chair, compared to some
other places we been.

Don't know where this bus is goin,' don't know
what kind of luck is blowin' our way.
All I know is, we done enough travelin'
we surely almost been there before.

(HURRICANE KATRINA 2005)

CARE

Nurture pours out in solitude
from a water hose over thirsty plants,
who would place no blame on neglect,
nor give thanks for my care.

Yet the yellow Butterfly flower
bows under my spray,
rewarding me with my own love:
as though an infant smiled at me
with her uncontrollable mouth.

The wrongs that haunt me, that dwell
in the space between stomach and heart,
are momentarily quelled in this sacramental act.
A seed of redemption
falls in a pool
at the flower's feet.

There is nothing to worship, nothing
but the minuscule red spots
        inside her yellow petals
                where butterflies feed.

DEAR GENERALS AND CORPORATIONS:

I've always wondered what it takes
to want to hold a gun —
to pull the trigger on someone
you don't even know.

My uncle had a room full of guns
and soul full of hate.
I always assumed that's what it takes.
His sons joined the army.
They ridiculed me at my wedding
for wanting to join the Peace Corp.
"What ya wanna do that for?!"
When I asked why they wanted to
fight in a foreign land, they said,
"To get rid of some communists,"
and laughed.

I didn't join the Peace Corp.
Neither of them had to fight.
Their army didn't win.
Communist men and women were absorbed
into the Institutional walls, while their old enemy —
the many opiates of the people —
took to the streets, so to speak.
My aged cousins are still behind the fight,
though the Hammer and Sickle have morphed
into a Crescent Moon.

They never were lovers of the land:
      Phoenix
            Redwood City
                  Charlottesville —
Measured in terms of convenience.

All equally possible.
Easy enough to leave behind
as long as you had your stuff
and a hope to get more.

Iraq is a big land, where
the Earth shows itself
to the People.
The Earth can be seductive.

You can love it so much
you will be jealous to share it.
Love takes up the guns of hate.

Here's something new, Dear Generals:

Send your boys home and teach them
to love the land they left behind.
To undress her of some pavement
and grow trees in its place.
Plant a "Victory Garden."
Harvest the sun.

For you will have won the entire planet
and come out rich.

MONOTONE

In a monotone the nuthatches nag me,
declaring a lazy afternoon with no crescendos.
Declare the end of endeavor, sever the ties
with making things better, the ties
with making things at all —
the ties of time.

For all is made already, and wants only to be heard.
In the beginning, there was only this tone,
only the Word, as the ancestors say.
And after all that trouble, it wants to be heard.

And there it goes, beginning again today.
The humming mud-daubers signal a need
to build nests in the eaves.
Even though it's been done before.

SINGLE MOTHER'S HOME

Spiders have freedom of the upper walls and ceilings;
children of the rambling floors,
where tricycles circle:
living room, family room, kitchen — zoom —
throughout the rainy days.

Second-hand sofas house clean laundry
in rumpled baskets and neat white stacks.

The kitchen table — a long rectangle —
happily shared by cereal bowls with
a bit of sweet milk in the bottom, crayons,
pages of children's art, homework, and, oddly,
ornate glass vases, whose beading makes
her third job.

Not only my grandmother would say:
"This place needs some attention."
But I would have to mention that
attention is given freely to children, and three jobs.
Messes are temporary intrusions on a tidy mind
and often find their way into art.

OLD AGE

The lizards I watch day after day,
year after year,
on the rocks, the compost,
foundation blocks, porches,
tell me about my losses.
On the first hot day, the black jackets come off
and scatter across their miniature landscapes,
       Empty.   Relaxed.
Not having to move, to hunt, to escape any more.

My heart crawls inside to bask
in the warm stillness of painless, taskless time.
The evening winds blow us away.
But my heart returns, heavy.
Pain returns, a burden.

The jackets do not return —
no longer prowl among the garden plants,
cooling themselves at the edge of the water.
They rest on the limbs of drying bushes,
waiting for another wind, and for insects
that may have been prey in another time
to consume the remaining cells.

HYPOTHERMIA

They found him lying in his own front yard
            naked, in twenty degrees,
the door wide open, heat turned off,
coffee frozen in his cup.
Clothes were strewn across the floor,
buttons ripped and scattered
in desperation.

The firemen said, at the extremes,
fire and ice feel the same on the body.

COTTONWOODS

They shed their furry seeds
this time of year, spreading them
as far as wind and fairy wings
can carry.
Seeing them makes me sneeze.

Each is a world of its own,
the entire genome of this being
which so greenly shelters us
from the western sun.

We mow the grass weekly.
It is grass, not a lawn.
So it holds the secret
beneath it —
underneath the buttercups, violets
grass and apple trees…

You must dig down to find the secret.
You won't get far
so then you must dig sideways.

It will take a long time
and it will reveal itself
slowly: the secret of
ubiquitous roots traveling under grass
making a nest of hardened snakes.

THE CAMELLIA

The full lust of fall blooms
along the river, in all stages of decay.
Cottonwoods, tenacious
since early spring, from the spreading
of its white soft clouds of seed,
trying to grow all over the garden,
and now, its sun-gold leaves
hang on against the wind
and rattle to its rhythm.

Locusts stand bare
of fragrant blossoms and yellow leaves,
which have scattered over the grass.
And on the other side, a blaze of coral
shouts from a foreign maple who
has made herself at home
in the river rocks and sand.

Meanwhile, in a dark corner of the yard,
the camellia secretly sets plump buds,
quietly making ready for spring,
imagining her own
luscious pink flowers.

ARTISTS

Salute the water and the wind,
those artists shaping clouds
into white forests of the sky —
into migrating beasts.
Praise those restless creators
who paint into a future downwind,
brushing my skin with stories upwind.

Water and Wind, twins intertwined,
inseparable in space and time,
who change the face of oceans and skies,
mountains, farms, cities, lives.

They draw the face of death out of hospitals
and into the streets of New Orleans.

(HURRICANE KATRINA 2005)

CELEBRATION

Frogs sing at a steady pulse,
crickets chirp high monotones
as Labor Day closes under a warm full moon.

The frogs stop — a large creature is passing by.
Buzzing night-bugs and the refrigerator
hum out of time. The daughter's boom-box
tries to regiment the scene.
Upstairs, the lights are out early
but the beds creak.
The first day of school is a lot like Christmas.
They can't sleep.

And what if there were no school
and no Christmas?
What if we worked and slept through
the ripening of blackberries, the
gathering of firewood,
the first rain to settle summer dust, the
Solstice and the Snow,
breathing changes in and out sans ceremony?

Would we awake simply to see
willows blooming in the creek
or a lizard race across a chunk of firewood?

MIMOSA

Cotton-candy blossoms almost touching, two trees
reach out to one another in a sort of minuet.
They exhale Desire, fairy-tale beauty and fragrance.

I want to be one of the butterflies,
a hummingbird, or a bee of a race
who can trace her way back
to this pinnacle of lust —
can year after year find her heart's desire.
Can know it for ten minutes a year
in her small eternity.

A human heart is consumed by desires
never satisfied — not even understood.
It is burdened by longings buried deep in primordial brains, which send
our hearts unwelcome adrenaline
attached to no fear of tigers or daggers.

Is it a vestige of our evolution, before Doubt
mounted its mighty campaign to inhabit the human heart?

We cannot exhale the Doubt
and we offer our pocketbooks to Desire.

Meanwhile, the Mimosa and her lovers
sow millions of children in wombs
woven in tidy pea-green pods,
into the riverside loam.

OLD WOMAN IN THE GARDEN

The high-pitched ring from the crown of a chickadee —
the very crown of the crown, where sound breaks through
into vast, intelligence blue —
fades in ripples,
mixes with the stuff of clouds,
falls to blend with the yellow April smells:
mustard and daffodil.

April opens its yellow genitalia
to the fuzzy golden ball
of a bumble bee.

And then, the crow breaks in,
his black laughter crashing on the scene
like a splash of cold water,
unequivocal and clean.

There, yellow youth is swallowed
in great gulps, by old grey lungs,
and crooked fingers brown with earth
plow around new spinach.

BLACKBERRIES

Fragrance was everywhere
in the ground, above the river, in the air
when we arrived in Hoopa from the draught of the south.
I didn't know that air had fragrance.
I was twenty-two. I stared hard into the lush-ness
looking for a source. A new kind of learning.
The world became new.
Wild plums grew in the yard — yellow and purple.
Green brambles crowded the roadsides.
The thorny brambles hid and protected
old secrets of this hidden valley:
foxes, rattlesnakes, eel, eight foot sturgeons
and *blackberries.*
Their darkness shone like jewels from the shadows of the bush.
Their fragrance lodged
in a new place my heart had grown.
Love at first sight, it was.
My arms bled for them. I couldn't stop.
I was pulled out. My man
didn't seem to understand.
I became a hunter-gatherer,
like any other Hupa woman.
I cooked them and they released
the full orgasm of their odor.
The tiny house was infused with love.
It's been fifty years, every one
made new again with the ripening of
blackberries.

part eight

VOICES

The voices in your head
        are really okay.
Let them tell their stories.
All you have to do
        is to make them tell the truth.
That is the hard part.
They are not talking about you,
        if you really listen.

I try not to be the hero,
or the most beloved, though
the temptation nips at my heels.
Fantasies can generate a sort of
        hormonal charge, but
they will let you down in the end.

I try to draw energy from the charge,
        but move on to truth —
through the memories and stories
I didn't understand back then.

THE SNAKE

The poor basil plant I am about to set into the ground
is root-bound.
Still, I dig the hole, drop it in,
run water over the serpentine tangle of roots,
hoping for a miracle. Hoping
it's not too close to the ever-spreading sage,
which I closely observe.
From under the branches
of that tough shrub comes
a watery movement, striped
in green, red, black.
It's flowing toward a leak in my hose.
Now the completed form is revealed
as it draws its tail out into the sun.

I say "Hello" and "Welcome to the garden."
Its red tongue shoots out like
blood from a syringe,
waving a flag of pride and menace.
So tiny, yet
I am not tempted to touch.

OTTER PEOPLE IN THE SUNSET

They see the opaque pearl-essence of the river's surface
from the under side.
With the sun at their backs, and vision enhanced,
they swim upstream after schools of steelhead.

Some are our brothers, you know.
The otter people are body-snatchers,
in case you didn't know.
We treat them with respect but
do not allow them to see us.
If they see you, they can take you —
turn you right into an otter person.
And so you remain, forever.

Unless you do them a favor and
they decide to return to your village.

I don't know why we worry about it so much.
They have a good life.
Nothing eats them.
They never starve.

THE PITCHER

My father's mother was less than five feet tall.
She was a proper Southern Baptist, a proper woman,
a proper share-cropper's wife.
She could guide a plow behind a mule as well as anyone else.
But she preferred to shovel the Texas dust off her wood floor
and to otherwise make a proper home.
She was most happy in her suburban California house later on.

She named my father "Billie" (not William).
When she pronounced his name, she wrinkled her nose slightly,
emphasizing the long "e" sound. "Beelee."
"Honey" is distinctly nasal and big on the short "u."

"Hunni, I want to give you this," holding the pitcher before her.
She reached inside and pulled out an old-fashioned handkerchief
and emptied into her hand a piece of old bread
with one bite missing.
"Hunni, this is the piece of toast Beelee was eating
when he was called up to the war. The man
told him to finish his breakfast, but Beelee said good-bye
and got up and left."

I'm sure my jaw dropped in amazement.
She wouldn't have noticed.
All I could say was, "It's a beautiful pitcher.
Where did it come from?"

Quietly.
"I think your granddad stole it from a motel room."

WHITECAPS

Midsummer whitecaps bounce gently downriver,
soothing a universe beneath
leaving
minerals, microbes, memories
for the mossy rocks below…
for the trilobites to feast, for the fishes to eat.
A month ago, they would have knocked you down
and kept on riding.

Now you can stand bare and let the worms living in duckweed
bite you on the ass.
If you wish.
My wish is to look down into the green water and see
all the human longings hiding among the mosses:
how they cling to the rocks abiding
all the slings and arrows of outrageous Spring.
And no matter the measure of Contentment —
impossible as the rocks to measure —
they cling to the surface of things.

THE LAST BOX

Five years after my father's death,
I steel my nerves for the last box —
pictures, postcards, funeral ledgers
of generations past,
names unfamiliar except as overheard
from those long gone.
Old Texas names: Geneva, Lankford, Dooley, Ila Mae.

The black and white pictures
distant, lacking definition, so I can't see
the features on faces.
All blood relatives
with stories:
The suicide of Beatrice after her husband died.
Geneva worked until death in her nineties.
W.T. was my Cherokee great-grandfather.
His face appears as a dark apparition. Featureless.

This box of unspoken history
means less to my children than it does to me.
It's fire season.
I can't build a ritual fire
to send the memories up in holy smoke.

The last box of someone's memories
heads for a landfill.

ODE TO SADNESS

Sadness can be worn like a ragged dress
or a club foot, or like leprosy.
It can be worn between narrowing brows
above a plea for mercy.

It can turn itself inside out like a sweater,
and hide behind laughing eyes, a mouth that
works hard at a smile.
It may not be worn at all and not even noticed
until all of its buttons break.

Tears are only temporary visits
from the "old friend" darkness, or
even one from joy.

Sadness screams through a torn screen door
in the house of poor repair.

THE SMELL OF SMOKE

Here at the bottom, on the river of this valley
it is easy to imagine the smell of smoke.

"Is that the barbecue?"
        "No."
"Are people next-door smoking, or burning illegally?"
        "No, it's a different kind of smoke."

One need not wait for the Evening News.

"The rocks across the river have a…yellowish look,
don't they?"
        "Yes, they do."

It happens every year nowadays.
From here, you may soon see large clouds
forming and taking the shape of
some kind of mushroom.
If you are lucky, you may see the stem
burst into flame.
Usually they start in places few people ever see:
on the steep slopes, narrow trails, serpentine cliffs,
and jewel lakes nestled in baskets of continuity,
made by the earth in her mountains.
Yet, for those who do walk in the High Country,
the flames still live in black scars on ancient trees,
having aged without human surveillance.

THE MARRIAGE OF MONARCHS

I planted milkweed to attract them to my yard
where I had never seen them.
To my amazement, they came.
And every year thereafter.

Now they appear in pairs, like couples
attending a grand cotillion in their
most extravagant attire.
They dance two by two in the air above
bee balm and echinacea, circling, chasing
in do-si-dos and allemandes:
a foreplay of deep orange and black
in exuberant attraction.

And before my eyes, the two become one,
as sometime occurs in a long loving marriage.

THE TEN THOUSAND BEINGS

Leaves on cottonwoods across the river are so many!
Spiders, ants, maple bugs, birds, squirrels
hunt among them, building nests, eating holes in the leaves.
They eat, and the trees make new heart-shaped leaves
year after year. The little hearts cover the ground in winter
breeding a new world of worms and microbes
beneath their moldering dankness.

Such abundance! Such fine-tuned sustenance!

Our own lives recede year after year.
It is a painful process.

But when it is finished
this abundance will remain.

THOR MAKES A STAND AGAINST APOLLO AND LUNA

Before the eclipse, the sun was a fluorescent
orange ball in a smoke-filled sky.
The river looked on fire
as the ball reflected on the water like flames.

This had nothing to do with the sun or moon.
This was about the Earth!
Forest fires burned in all directions.
Smoke thickened like gravy overhead.

The temperature dropped by twenty degrees.
Pre-dawn darkness persisted past ten o'clock,
when, apparently, somewhere a solar eclipse
was observed through special sunglasses
on thousands of faces.
It changed nothing.

The fires turned most of the Kalmiopsis forest
into charcoal.

Lightning lies closer to home than the sun or moon.

SPIDER SILK

Fine lines of spider silk lace the October air,
mostly unseen.
But they are there
to the always-staring eye:
a barely visible universe of hunters and hunted.

The old Spider Grandmother,
wise character of Hopi history,
takes care of the Earth in her unassuming manner:
managing the insect world
in ways Monsanto couldn't imagine.

She is endlessly extending connections
between all the mountains
and strengthening the ties that bind them.
People in New Guinea make fishing nets
from her silk. Somewhere else in the world
there is a bridge woven from it
that people trust to walk upon:
stronger than steel, I hear.

She invented the concept of Web.
(Sorry, Mr. Gore.)
The Many connected in this way —
mountain to mountain — are stronger
than any one point.

Villagers still live high in the mountains,
driven up-slope by their enemies
back in the times when women
wove medicine out of plants
and tended to Wisdom.
Their views of the World are
remarkably similar.

If there is any sense to my life,
I sometimes see it in threads
the Spider has woven every which way
with her own wisdom.
I don't think she wonders what to do next.

Her web has no ending.
I see that I still must live my life,
and that there is room for it on the outer-most strand.

I feel that I can start spinning again.

THANKSGIVING

Yellow-gold leaves cover the grass
like a blanket over the year.
I am thankful that it covers no tragedies
close to me.
Apple trees and mimosas hang on to their dresses,
waiting for the next wind, or a freeze,
or in case something else needs covering.

I am betting against a freeze this year.
It is getting warmer here, an event
that is scantly covered, like the grass,
and not especially dreaded
in this particular location.
This is not the same river or
the same grass, not the same leaves
or the same air.

So a year, whenever you want it to begin,
isn't a repetition of the last
even in old age.

AFTER THE "PULL DATE"

If it is, don't buy it.
Some things are okay, You and I,
for example. But only "OK."
They can survive, but live in
a smaller part of the world
than the ones that are not yet expired.

Some of the meaty, more muscular ones
either wear a guise of healthy preservatives
or were just better
in the beginning, before
the crescendo collapsed like
a piece of bone collapsing on a nerve.

We survivors avoid looking at our cell phones
and startle when they ring.
Can they really show us the way to get home?

AN OFFERING

Here in the land of wild azaleas and darlingtonia,
fragrance moves down my body until
I feel like new love.
Roots spread through me downward
into the Siskiyou soil.
Yes, a special place.

The snowy peaks not so far away
stand strong against a late spring sky.
They are shouting to me!

"We have seen you before, Old Woman!
You huffed and puffed up our slopes and
across our monkey-flower meadows.
Swam joyously in our jewel lakes!
We are happy to see you still walking the earth."

I fill not with regret at my frailty,
nor longing for what is lost.

Not this time. This time
I fill with gratitude for what has been,
and still is, somewhere.

Nostalgia frequently lies like a fog
over true memories buried deep in gray matter.

Thank you, my giant friends,
for offering me a true memory out of the fog!

CREDITS AND ACKNOWLEDGEMENTS

I wish to give special thanks to my father, Bill Davis. He was an English teacher and the one who got me interested in writing.

Also, thanks to Michael Spring, the inspiring contemporary poet who has encouraged me and conveyed to me that I could write poetry worth reading.

Numerous poems in this collection have appeared in the following publications: *The Amethyst Review, Blue Moon Cafe Review, Cobra Lily: a review of Southwest Oregon literature & art, Illinois Valley News, Isacoutstic, Pulsar, Strange Butterflies, Takilma Common Ground, The Writers' Cafe Magazine, Turtle Island Quarterly*, and *Unbirthing*.

ABOUT THE AUTHOR

Coreen Davis Hampson has lived in Southern Oregon since 1972. That was a year in which many idealistic urbanites moved here to live off the land, frequently communally. After graduating from Los Angeles State University with a B.A. in Anthropology, she decided to be a farmer. She and three friends started a farm in Selma. She has maintained a passion for growing things from the earth to this day, at age 73.

This is her first book of any kind, though she has also nurtured a passion for poetry and song from an early age. She writes regularly and is currently working on family stories for her grandchildren. She plays "old time music" with husband Scott Hampson and other friends. From 1975 until 2007, she played in local bands such as The Bitterlick String Band, The Generic String Band (for contradances), Heartstrings, and Uncle Fluster. In 2009, she wrote a CD of songs about gardening for the "Farm-to-School" project and recorded it with three children from the Illinois Valley.

Coreen's poetry reflects her love and fascination with the natural world, as well as her love of music and metaphor.